PERSONAL RICHES AND ENTREPRENEURSHIP

Thoughts and Ideas of Owning a Family Business

By Matthew D. Mohr

Dacotah Paper Co.
Copyright © 2001

Library of Congress Control Number: 2001087828
ISBN 0-9709251-0-7
MG
Printed in the United States of America

Additional copies may be ordered from:

Dacotah Paper Co.

P.O. Box 2727

Fargo, ND 58102

(800) 323-7683

DEDICATION

For: Benjamin
       Caleb
       and Berea

May you all have richly rewarding lives. Your
unconditional love has given me great
personal riches, and makes me proud to be
your father.

ACKNOWLEGEMENTS

Through the years of my life, many people have affected me and helped me to grow to become the person I am today. My appreciation extends first to my loving parents, Marcia and Fred Mohr.

To Mrs. Joan Humphrey, my caring and patient high school teacher, who spent countless early morning hours with me encouraging me to believe in myself. My admiration goes to William Gerdes, Jim Hansen, Melinda Kramer, and Wilbur Lewellen, the four university instructors who showed me how to be the best.

A special thanks to Jim Alexy, Mark Biebelheimer, Mayor Bruce Furness, Jim Gargiulo, Emily Hagen, John Hertsgaard, Mary Lindgren, Kathy Lindvig, Steve Ruppel, David Silbergleit, Deborah Soliah, Carolyn Songey, Jon Strinden, Jim Wieland, and Bob and Jane White, my cherished friends who have always inspired me to achieve success.

Special accolades to the many doctors, nurses, and therapists at MeritCare Hospital in Fargo who guided me in my recovery.

For the support of Alison Nowacki, who typed and retyped this book's manuscript without a single complaint. To all the great employees of Dacotah Paper Co., past and present, who have supported me, and who have accepted my and my family's many shortcomings, allowing our company to grow and prosper for nearly a century.

Table of Contents

Chapter 1

MY STORY

I am the president and Chairman of the Board of Dacotah Paper Co., a successful wholesale distribution company based in Fargo, North Dakota. My family has owned the business since 1960. The business was established in 1906. Dacotah Paper Co. is a 120 employee industrial paper wholesaler serving all of North Dakota, Minnesota, and parts of Wisconsin, South Dakota, and Montana.

In addition to my duties at Dacotah Paper Co., I am employed as an instructor of entrepreneurship for the College of Business at North Dakota State University.

The year 1998 began as most years. I spent time reviewing my accomplishments of the previous year, and began writing my plans and goals for the future. For some reason I reviewed my last 20 years of goal planning sheets. I stated to my wife I was struggling to establish large or significant new goals since I had achieved nearly every major goal I had set over the past 20 years. My life was grand and in good balance. I had a great family, and my health was seemingly perfect. My career was stimulating, fun, and rewarding. I was teaching Sunday School and felt I was spiritually strong. Financially I was secure. Mentally I continued to read and grow beyond my formal education. Needless to say, I did not expect to face the challenges I would endure the following months.

On March 20, 1998, I suffered a massive stroke and subsequently spent seven weeks in the hospital, which gave me some time to prepare writing this book and forced me to think of what value there was in having my own family business.

A stroke affects each person in different ways. Essentially, a stroke is caused either by a blood clot which blocks blood flow to the brain, or the bursting of a blood vessel in the brain, which eliminates proper blood flow to the brain. In each case, the victim faces some level of brain damage. My particular stroke was caused by a blood clot which resulted in a major stroke. We were lead to believe, at the time of my hospital admission, that I might not be able to walk or work again. For the rest of the book, you will find some new insight to what the requirements and joys of being an entrepreneur are, what the word riches may mean, and what value lies in owning and/or pursuing your own family business empire, as well as gaining a good perspective of the value of persevering through a crisis as a family.

Chapter 2

THE HOSPITAL

Seven weeks in a hospital are not a joyous experience for anyone. For a highly motivated, energetic, physically active man, those seven weeks were a nightmare. I was vice-chairman of the board of the hospital's foundation, and specifically asked my family not to use my position with the hospital to achieve adjustments in my care; though, in retrospect, I did seem to be assigned the more well-liked and professional staff.

I had no idea what having a stroke meant. When I first regained consciousness and was told of my ailment, I thought to myself: I had a stroke, no big deal. I'm me, I'll just hop out of this hospital and life will be normal again. Little did I know my body's left side was completely paralyzed, my brain had undergone tremendous trauma, and what appeared to be clear thinking was often cloudy thoughts. I was lucky that my ability to comprehend events and issues was still relatively strong, although initially my body's malfunctioning did frustrate me, and I was not able to initially grasp the idea of being a hemiplegic.

The days in the hospital dragged on, the nights were torture. My normal day in the hospital started with breakfast, then to speech therapy, on from speech therapy to physical therapy and occupational therapy, lunch; then in the afternoon therapy started all over. Evening meals were often taken in my room. Fortunately, my loving mother had the strength and time to sit with me each night as I struggled to fall asleep. Without my mother's company, I am not sure how I could have survived each night.

I was very frustrated not having my mobility. One particular day, at my request, Brad Arett, my primary day nurse, was connecting my room phone. I saw my opportunity to prove myself. I slowly unhooked myself from the wheelchair. Brad saw me and caught me before I tried to take a step. Rather than berate me, he laughed with me and encouraged me to wait. I frequently see Brad in the hospital now when I am visiting. He always has a smile and encouraging words. This is just one example of my good fortune with people who cared for me. Believing someone truly cares is a source of great personal richness. Thankfully, Brad was there to help me and encourage me through my hospital stay.

My primary physical therapist, Norlene Tracy, has a Masters Degree in Physical Therapy. Day after day she would work with me, having to keep me awake, teaching me how to relearn to walk and then how to climb stairs. Sometimes I felt she was frustrated by not providing a faster recovery for me. She would try new ideas to help challenge me to work harder. It was Norlene who eventually took me to a gym to start my independent routine.

Early one morning as I sat in my wheelchair, I observed other patients re-learning to walk. I thought and prayed to myself, "God, please let me take some steps again." Finally, one Saturday morning, Christi Teigen, a physical therapist, tried a new approach and I took a step. As time progressed, I re-learned walking independently. Norlene would constantly encourage me to keep working. The day she and I went for a walk on the grass outside together was a happy day for both of us. After I was walking, Norlene admitted one morning that she wasn't sure I would progress to this level of independence. My reply to her was, "You didn't know Matthew Mohr."

Sarah Honea Ring, my speech language pathologist, was a salvation; one of the few people besides Brad, my nurse, I felt truly wanted me to succeed, and someone who believed in me. She listened for hours to my "philosophy" and encouraged me to grow while teaching me how to strengthen my speech abilities. Session after session she would laugh with me, listen, and encourage me to forge ahead. Had it not been for her great positive attitude and wonderful encouragement, I am certain my recovery would have taken much longer. To this day I feel a great deal of gratitude toward her, and thankfulness for her help. Sarah is one of those unique people who opens doors of optimism for other people through her love and her natural ability to inspire people to achieve.

Occupational therapy deals with getting back to the tasks of daily life. Fortunately for me, our hospital had just added a driving rehabilitation program; the foundation board, of which I was a member, funded the program. My primary occupational therapist, Lia Dobrinz, was a key member of the driving team, so she felt a level of gratitude towards my role and put forth extra effort with my occupational rehabilitation. Due to the extent of my brain injury, my doctor felt compelled to notify the state, and at his recommendation my driver's license was revoked. Loosing my driver's license was a frustrating experience. I was accident-free and ticket-free for many years. In early August of 1998, I re-took and passed the written portion of the North Dakota Driver's test; then I enrolled in the hospital's driver's rehabilitation program. Lia spent hours encouraging me to build my driving skills. I re-took the driving portion of the test in late August 1998, only one month after starting the hospital driver's rehabilitation program (scoring better this time than I did when I first passed the test at 15 years old!). One year after re-taking the driver's test, I remained accident free and ticket free - a further tribute to Lia's teaching ability.

As I regained my strength, I fought to return to work. My first days back in the office were in a wheelchair. My co-workers offered much encouragement. Without my drive to be back to work, I wonder how fast my recovery would have been. My best days, initially, occurred when I was in the office.

I am lucky that our computer people are very adept at providing good working systems. Shortly after returning home, we set up a virtual office in my home so I could be in constant contact with our business. I believe this helped me recover quicker and return to the office much faster.

As my rehabilitation continues, I feel compelled to rebuild my strength. I am at the office every day of the normal work week, including some Saturdays. I have been very fortunate achieving great success in my rehabilitation, and I expect to return to a level of physical vitality which is close to my previous or pre-stroke condition. After being on my own for a few months, I contacted Christi Teigen, one of my physical therapists, who very generously offered her own personal free time to review my gym routine. She was very encouraging and provided new ideas to help me succeed quicker.

I am constantly thankful I am part of a family business. I suggest to myself; where else could I work any time I want, define my work hours, and allow myself three sessions per week in the gym for my personal re-training? In addition to the gym time, there are countless doctor appointments as I struggle to resolve the many issues my body faces during this time of rebuilding. Only as the owner of a family business could I be employed and maintain such a variable schedule. Although my three weekly sessions in the gym give me time to think creatively, the gym time also provides me the opportunity to listen to audio business programs. Of course, my commitment and drive to be involved with the business is evident each day, whereas many people would choose their disability checks. Yet, for me, working is a great personal motivator. I still love to be at the office each and every day.

Chapter 3

THE EXCURSIONS

As part of the rehabilitation program, my hospital employs recreational therapists. The recreational therapists are supposed to assist patients in safely returning to non-employment related activities.

My first excursion was to join with a group of other patients and go to a movie. My mother joined as my escort. It was probably the first movie my mother and I had gone to for 30 or more years. We loaded up into a hospital van and were driven to the theater. Most of us were in wheel chairs. Due to concern about my ability to swallow, it was suggested I not have any popcorn. It was nice to get out of the hospital, and I was very thankful for my mother's company. I felt blessed to have my mother so willing to be with me. I missed popcorn, and not having any emphasized my loss of control over my life.

The second organized excursion in which I was able to participate was a trip to the local shopping mall. We were given a choice of where we wanted to eat our meal. We were given a spending limit for our food cost; beyond that, we needed to bring our own money. It was then I realized how much control of my life I had lost. My wallet had gone home with my wife; together we would determine how much I could take along. Being the master of my own finances, I never before had someone place me on spending limits. We decided on some cash and a credit card. For my meal I chose to have Chinese. Willy, another stroke patient, also chose Chinese. Willy and I had become friends in a nice way at the hospital. Willy is a classic western North Dakota rancher. He owns a rather large ranch which he works with his wife and family. A strong, rugged, friendly, cowboy sort of man. When I think of him, I picture him tossing hay bales around like they weighed but a few pounds. Outside of our friendly outgoing personalities, Willy and I were quite different. He is a western North Dakota rancher, I am the classic eastern North Dakota businessman.

For our mall excursion, each of us needed a hospital escort. Sarah, my speech language pathologist, joined as my escort.

As we bought our meals, it turned out that Willy and I purchased (unknowingly) exactly the same meals. Our friendship strengthened. After dinner it was time to shop.

I owned part of a young women's retail store called Vanity. We happened to have a store in the particular mall we were visiting. I asked Sarah to walk me down to the store so I could check things out. Slowly we made our way to the young women's clothing store. Willy and his escort followed. I went through the store proudly pointing out all the nicer things to Sarah. To my surprise, Willy had followed into the store. One moment I turned around to find Willy watching me in total disbelief.

Willy looked totally stunned (I'm sure he thought I was in much worse shape mentally than it seemed in the hospital). This bigger than life rancher's "little buddy" had truly lost his mind and was shopping for women's clothes for himself! Today, I chuckle every time I remember the experience, realizing Willy had no idea I owned part of the store. Despite my encouragement, Sarah never took me up on my offer to buy her anything in the store. Hospital policy forbids therapists from accepting material gifts from patients.

Chapter 4

EMOTIONS RUN WILD

One consequence of many strokes is an imbalance to the person's emotional state. I had always been as "solid as a rock." Unfortunately for many stroke victims, they become unstable at times. Some experience vocabulary (typically swearing) changes, some find themselves saying very inappropriate things to and about other people. Some cry without warning or reason. Crying is referred to as reflex crying. My emotional imbalance was to cry at seemingly normal events in life. The first Sunday I was able to attend church, I cried. One day my wife and I visited my childhood grade school. Again, I cried for seemingly no reason. Later I learned of the phenomenon of reflex crying. Once I understood what was happening, I became much more stable emotionally. Yet, I still feel I have to be respectful of the potentially explosive emotional reaction I could have to any given experience.

Chapter 5

A SCARY VISIT TO E.R.

One early Monday I had gone to the gym in the morning as I normally do. That afternoon as I made my way to the office, I found my chest hurting and I had a hard time breathing. I drove myself to the emergency room, arriving about 2:30 P.M. At 4:00, I suggested to the nurse I felt good enough to go home, but she insisted I wait for the E.R. doctor.

Shortly before 5:00 P.M. I was hooked up for an EKG, then chest X-rays were taken. Around 6:00 P.M. I was asked to lie down and wait for the test results. The doctor then ordered blood tests. I was told of the blood test order, and my minister walked in to say hello to me. I thought to myself, this must be the end; my minister is here to give me my last rights! Actually, another member of our congregation was in the E.R. at the same time, and my minister had been called to visit, so learning I was in the E.R. he thought he should see both of us.

A nurse walked in around 6:15 P.M. asking, "Does anyone know you are here?" I told the nurse I had called my wife and not to worry. She left briefly and returned asking, "Are you sure you don't want us to call your mother or your wife right now?" I had no idea what was going on. My wife called expressing worry and I became emotional. I began to think I would never see my family again!

18

A Scary Visit To E.R.

Finally, around 6:30 P.M. I flagged someone down and asked them to find a person who could let me know what was going on. The doctor responded, informing me all was well with the tests so far, but he wanted to wait for the results from the blood tests just to be sure. The blood tests came back fine.

Shortly before 7:00 P.M. the doctor informed me he felt there was nothing wrong, discharging me with well-wishes. As I drove home in the dark, I cried all the way hoping all was truly well. When I arrived home, I hugged my children and shed tears of joy knowing I had some time left with them after all.

Chapter 6

WHAT IS RICH?

Everyone has a different opinion of what rich means to them. To some it is how many pennies they may accumulate in a bank account, to others it's how big their brokerage account looks to the stock broker. Some perceive rich in terms of health, family, happiness, etc. To others it is having life filled with things they want or desire.

According to my copy of Webster's Dictionary, rich means "having abundant possessions and especially material wealth." Note the focus on material things. Being rich in our world today is having a life in which you enjoy an internal feeling of joy or the feeling of positive well-being. To be rich, you not only need things, but you need personal time, friends, love, faith, and the belief in yourself. When you are rich, you realize that regardless of the circumstances you face, you have the faith to lead a rewarding and enjoyable life.

My seven weeks in a hospital bed are an excellent example of finding myself in a circumstance which I did not anticipate. Regardless of my material wealth, I was hospital bound. Yet, my family enterprise allowed me personal riches. For seven weeks my mother stayed by my side night after endless night. Our family business provided her the time and financial resources to be near me at my time of need.

20

My wife faced little financial distress, and maintained our household in my absence.

It was perhaps my mother's undaunted love and devotion which prompted me to try to define rich myself. I am convinced without a doubt, if I had millions of extra dollars available, my care would not have changed at all during my hospital stay. To my caregivers, additional compensation would not have created a better environment for me. My nurse, Brad, did not save me from falling because of the money he earned, nor did my therapists determine the level of help they provided me based on their paychecks. Each, I feel, gave me their best efforts and worked hard with me to help me recover as fast as possible.

With such financial resources, I may very well have moved the hospital to my home. Yet, I now know that the best place for me was in the hospital. My richness during those trying weeks came from my family and friends who visited me, the new friends I made in the hospital, and my belief I would conquer this unexpected adversity to lead a productive, joyful life again.

Chapter 7

THE FAMILY BUSINESS EMPIRE BUILDING ERA

There is a revolution sweeping the United States today. Hundreds of people are getting involved with their own family businesses. Some new entrepreneurs are starting by buying a franchise, some are starting new ventures totally on their own. Most are starting them without a clue of defining what their goals are or what they wish to accomplish by having their own family business.

From this new era I believe will dawn a new understanding, a new perspective and a new set of values. The current generation quickly learned those with the most toys did not have the best lives. Quality of life suffered too much. Now a redefining of the value of life is occurring. Freedom to choose, time for family, and healthy life habits have become driving forces. The current generation of business professionals are assessing their lives and asking how they can live better. Climbing the corporate ladder is not success any more. Having time, resources, and a loving family appear more rewarding. Yet, few of the new entrepreneurs have written family plans, let alone written business achievement objectives. It's no wonder the Mister and Misses This or That keep failing; they are owned with no objective but to be "successful" or the "to be my own boss" syndrome.

The Family Business Empire Building Era

A good friend of mine, working for a major multi-national company, decided to go into the haircutting-franchise business. He had great expectations of expansion and financial success, yet he quickly admits he had no idea how to work with the ever-changing personalities of his employees. He found himself pressured for time and stretched for understanding, resulting in business failure, but great learning for him. Had he worked to understand the employees and tried to create an environment which helped them grow and achieve their objectives in life, and if he would have written down why he was in the haircutting business, perhaps he could have communicated his dream to his employees and reached his dream by helping them achieve their dreams. My guess is, if he ever ventures out on his own again, I'm sure he'll do reasonably well; his first experience and its failure will turn out to be invaluable to him.

Employment gives a person a sense of purpose and helps create a sense of self worth. Being an entrepreneur gives a person concrete opportunities to help others achieve and grow in life.

There are hundreds of examples of very successful family enterprises. Most successful family enterprises carry with them strong core values such as honesty, integrity, fairness with employees, and a hard-working attitude. If you have a chance to learn about the great chocolate empires built by the Hershey family and the story of the Mars brothers, their stories are amazing. Reading the story of

The Family Business Empire Building Era

Napoleon Hill provides a unique perspective of a celebrated success story. Yet, few realize all the challenges Hill faced in his life. Abraham Lincoln's life is a tribute to positive tenacity.

The life of Napoleon Hill is a tremendous example of a hard-working, but unfocused entrepreneur. Hill faced many adversities and achieved greatness in our society, but frequently missed the achievement of the true riches in life. Reading Hill's life story is a lesson in life for anyone wishing to achieve success.

True entrepreneurs love their business and enjoy their every moment on the job. There is no defined work day or work week for the real entrepreneur. His or her life is filled with a passion and a drive for business success.

Being gainfully employed is a desirable station in life, but becoming a workaholic is not necessary for enjoyment or success. As an entrepreneur who truly loves his business, I know a place you call your own can have a major positive impact on your life. My personal sense of well being, my feeling of personal richness is greatly enhanced by my business enterprise.

Chapter 8

DEFINING YOUR PURPOSE

The reasons for starting out on your own are many, and vary by each individual. Unfortunately, too many new entrepreneurs have little purpose in mind as they venture out on their own. A new business enterprise captures the essence of goal setting. You must have meaningful and specific goals. What real purpose will your business serve on the economic landscape? What customers do you seek to serve? In what geographic territory do you plan to have your business located? Do you have enough customers to be successful there? It is essential to draft a written business plan complete with product, services to be sold, marketing plans, and financial projections.

One component necessary for successfully enlisting people to work with you is to be able to articulate your purpose and help the people achieve their dreams.

Simply defining your purpose as being a good dentist pales in comparison to being a business owner who succeeds through helping 200 people per month maintain a lifetime of pain free use of their own teeth. Which of these two definitions would you judge to appear more inspiring to a potential employee?

Defining Your Purpose

The Reverend Robert Schuller proclaims, "There is no such thing as a money problem, only an idea problem!" For the right idea, money, people, and the necessary resources will follow.

Chapter 9

SELF-DISCIPLINE

Most successful people have a high level of self-discipline. They have the ability to keep working on a project or keep striving to achieve a goal even though it seems impossible.

One of the big ingredients to the feeling of personal well-being or riches is the ability to exercise self-discipline.

It isn't fun for me to continue to go to the gym three times each week. I would much rather sleep in. But I get out of bed and go to the gym most mornings before sunrise.

Do you want to build a stock portfolio? It takes self-discipline. Give up the extra value meal for lunch, brown bag it. Maybe a few co-workers will think that you are odd, but in ten years these same people will wonder why your life is so much easier than theirs. How did you figure out how to save so much money when they are broke? Self-discipline and eliminating some of the low value, quick fixes (instant gratification temptations) will help you succeed.

I believe one of the big ingredients to the feeling of personal well-being or riches is the ability to exercise self-discipline.

Self-Discipline

The ball game is on, and it's Monday night. Do you grab a bag of chips and watch the game, or do you sit at your desk to rework your financial projections. Either option will take up about the same amount of time. Obviously, only the second option will bring you closer to the success you desire. Only one of these options takes self-discipline. The more you feel you deserve free time in your own mind, the less likely it is you are exercising the self-discipline to become successful.

Accomplishment, success, and personal riches flow to those who don't quit.

Chapter 10

STAY WITH IT

Some people grow to resent the word and the associated definition of having tenacity. The generation which won us World War II was filled with tenacious people. Had Eisenhower or Churchill not possessed great tenacity, our world would be much different from how we know it today. These great leaders had men and women who believed in them and both garnered the support of their countries. We went into a war for our freedom.

People fought for life and liberty. When the soldiers returned home, they built businesses, homes, schools, and hospitals with the same vigor and determination that was used to win the war. Today we all benefit from this generation's success. A generation with a great desire to succeed, win, and prosper. When facing the German Army, our soldiers did not desert; they all fought to win!

Contrast this generation with the next generation of workers – those too often in and out of jobs. From the hippies of the 60's to the Me Generation of the 70's and 80's. The quick fix and give-it-up attitude prevails today. Divorce is higher than ever. So is personal bankruptcy. Now we have created Generation X whose single most important question is, "What is in it for me?" A new generation growing up far too often in single parent homes, with parents who run from work and feel justified not working since they blame much of their personal failures on their parents having substituted work for family.

As a business owner, and a man working to rebuild his body, I feel gifted with an unusual level of stick-to-it-ness. In most every significant endeavor, I have been referred to as being very tenacious. Of course, I feel rich when I succeed. Much of my personal success has not come from intelligence or luck, but because I've always assessed the competition and simply out-worked them. Perhaps this attitude cost me my health, but my sense of personal riches has been greatly enhanced by this tenacity within me.

At Dacotah Paper Co., people are not given raises, they must earn them. It is easy to identify a success in our organization; ours or any organization for that matter. You just find the person who works the hardest or smartest and gets the most done!

What man or woman can really feel rich when they have not contributed to society or given the most to life by using their God-given talents?

Chapter 11

TALENTS

Most people know of the Bible story of the three men and their talents. I will not repeat it here, but rather choose a couple of modern-day talent stories.

In business, many employees feel entitled to the same rewards regardless of the efforts put forth and their actual accomplishments.   Part of this belief starts with our school system.

I love teaching. It allows me to share my knowledge, and I learn during the classes. In the Fall of 2000, two of my students who received a grade of B expressed the opinion they should have received an A.   One major part of their arguments were they attended each class, not missing one day. Surely, they felt, zero absences warranted the grade of A. Unfortunately, I do not believe showing up entails a person to the top reward. I did my best to tactfully explain that, in my class, it is what you produce when you show up, not just the fact you showed up which counts. Previous to my experience, these students had learned perfect attendance was the best to expect.   Their quality of performance was never judged until my class.

A more business related parable: Imagine you sell floor scrubbers.   You have three employees.   A customer calls you complaining about his floor machine not working as expected. You call in the first employee to explain you need him to investigate why the customer is not happy. About 30 minutes later this employee returns to your office and reports to you that he called the customer, talked to the receptionist, and was told the floor looked about normal, which was fine. Consequently, he thanked the receptionist and felt nothing else needed to be done.

After a few minutes you called in your second employee and explained to her that you needed her to investigate why the customer is not happy. About one hour later she returns to your office, telling you she took the company van, despite the rainstorm, to the customer's business, and looked over the floor, which was quite dirty due to all the mud being tracked in because of the rainstorm. Seeing the mud on the floor, she suggested to the customer that a new floor mat would solve the customer's problem, and sold the customer a new mat for a $25.00 profit. By now you think the second employee is an excellent employee.

Next you call in the third employee and explain to her that you need her to investigate why the customer is not happy. About 5:30 P.M. that evening the third employee gives you her report. She called the business that complained and questioned the receptionist. After thinking about what the receptionist meant by the description of the floor looking normal, she then took the company van, drove to the customer, and inspected the floor, which was dirty from the mud being tracked in due to the morning rainstorm. She then went to the equipment room, found the scrubber, detected a hose was plugged, and then learned that the customer's janitor couldn't lift the water tank out of the scrubber to change the water. After unplugging the hose and changing the water, the scrubber worked fine. It was the customer's janitor's problem. She then drove back to the shop, took out a smaller scrubber, and sold it to the customer for a $300.00 profit. She said she would have been back at 5:00 in time to leave, but she decided to stop to get the van washed so it was clean the next morning for deliveries.

Which of the three is more valuable? In most cases, all three employees feel they each did their jobs correctly, but, obviously, the third employee is worth more to have on staff, so the third employee should be compensated for higher value.

Most people think they are always doing their best, and feel they are entitled to superior rewards. The key to successfully leading an organization is determining those few who really produce superior results.

Just like school classes, not everyone should receive an A for showing up. Compensation is a hard decision, yet providing rewards for true performance is a thrilling experience. By helping people grow and achieve their best, will help you create a great feeling of richness within yourself. Only best performers deserve to win.

Chapter 12

YOUR BEST TURNS TO WINNING

As my children grow, I have tried to instill within them winning is fun and important, but it is more important to give your very best to everything you attempt. A half-hearted effort will usually result in failure. When you do your very best, you can go to sleep at night feeling rich. And as the rewards follow, as they usually do, you can use these rewards to enhance your life and the life of others, which will lead to a greater feeling of personal well-being.

In your life as an entrepreneur, you will find the people who always do their very best will become keys to your success. Much of life is personal friendships and special relationships; those who give you their best become your best friends. Do less than your best and it is a fast road to mediocracy.

Winning is very important. Life is filled with winning and losing, but most anyone feels best when they work hard to succeed and, as a result, enter the winner's circle. Few people or no one will cheer for the sloppy, lazy, uninterested contestant who doesn't give life their best.

Imagine the story of David and Goliath if David were to have faced the giant afraid and with cowardice. Undoubtedly, our world would be much different had Goliath won.

When America entered World War II, we went in to win the war for freedom. Would the world be filled with prosperity today if Hitler's armies would have prevailed?

Perhaps my own father spent too much time at work, but I loved him nonetheless. Maybe my childhood suffered because of his work. Maybe my life was enhanced by it. Without his drive to succeed, I would not enjoy my personal riches today. My father served in World War II. He saw the devastation caused by failure. He returned to America to succeed, and I'm thankful he worked to build the business I am blessed with today.

Chapter 13

MEDIOCRACY

I've never met a good parent who wanted their children to be average. Yet, too many adults settle for a mediocre life or settle for an average living. Why do we want great things from our children but not ask of great things from ourselves? I observe so many average performers in our society who think they should be paid top salary for average work.

Achieving, earning your way to success, is a powerful experience. Achievement leads to a great feeling of personal well-being. I have never met a person who truly wanted to be referred to as average.

When teaching, as students work to better understand the material, the teacher's and student's sense of success and riches is enhanced when the students finally achieve understanding. That great positive feeling when the light finally comes on adds greatly to the educational experience. Through work, tenacity, stick-to-it-ness, achievements, happiness, and personal riches flow to the top of society.

If you want the best, you need to be the best you can be.

Chapter 14

DIVERSIFIED INTERESTS

Most people have heard the old saying - you need to stick to your knitting. This is often interpreted to mean a business person should do only one thing. Certainly, you need to focus your energy; do one thing extremely well. However, by limiting your business pursuits, you will miss too much opportunity.

I am fortunate to lead a fantastic organization. Most of my energy is focused on how to better serve our customers and to grow our business. However, I enjoy becoming involved with other business endeavors. I feel these extra-curricular businesses strengthen my ability to lead Dacotah Paper Co., and provide me insight on how to better serve our diverse customer needs.

When presented with business plans, I always welcome the chance to review the plans. Sometimes I become involved, sometimes not; yet I always gain knowledge and learn new ways to enhance my primary profession.

A perfect example of how an "outside" business interest helped my primary company occurred in 1996 when I formed a group of local business owners and we became venture capitalists. We discovered Vanity, a locally owned young women's retail clothing operation, which was struggling and we bought it. It's hard to imagine two more different businesses than young women's clothing and industrial paper distribution. Vanity had around 2,500 employees and 160 stores all across the country. Dacotah Paper Co. at the time had 110 employees, one primary facility, and served one region (four states).

The originators of Vanity probably taught me more than the management team in place during my groups' ownership. Emery and Ann Jahnke, the originators of Vanity, are probably two of North Dakota's greatest entrepreneurs. Growing the business from one little rural shop to 160 stores and over $80 million in sales is a major accomplishment. It took me nearly two years to realize that it was the drive of these entrepreneurs that created this great business. Regardless of their management style, the employees respected the couple. In their efforts to grow, Emery and Ann employed some professional management which didn't recognize the original owners' leadership. The professional management started to influence and help standardize part of the business operations, which was necessary, but the employees started to loose their sense of relationship with Emery and Ann. As time went on, the business lost ground. Perpetuation of the family involvement in this business would have been a great boost toward greater success before Emery and Ann decided to retire.

As we struggled through the first year of owning Vanity, my partners and I became restless and started questioning more of the answers we received for lack of performance by the management group. At the close of the first year, I called the company president and said to him, "You've got one more year, it's time you let us know what you need to have to succeed, you can't blame any more problems on anyone else. You are in charge and we hold you accountable for the business success and failure." Happily, in January 1999, my partners and I sold our interests in this venture. It wasn't surprising that the venture group didn't always agree with the management group (who all had ownership interests). Each in the venture group came from a business where they made the daily decisions. As entrepreneurs, we were used to taking immediate action and expected the same attitude from the professional managers. Today, many of our proposed ideas have taken shape – it just took a little more time than we anticipated. The business is on track to grow and expected to do well again, but now it's primary owner is a successful businessman, and he is involved directly with decisions on how to operate the business.

A part of true retail success involves developing the right advertising tools to draw customers into your store. Meeting after meeting at Vanity we missed this basic marketing principle. As a result of this experience, I refocused Dacotah Paper Co.'s efforts and expenditures on advertising. It was a good gain for Dacotah Paper Co. due to this outside activity, and lead to a better understanding of advertising for me.

I recount this experience to demonstrate that without the experience I would have been a weaker leader. Fortunately, I have never blamed my lack of success on someone or something else. I have always accepted total responsibility for everything which happens at Dacotah Paper Co. and in my life. I think this fact has helped my leadership position. Everyone associated with Dacotah Paper Co. knows I hold myself accountable.

The Vanity experience helped teach me that a true entrepreneur has a burning desire to see his business succeed. Work is fun for the entrepreneur. For the true entrepreneur, the numbers represent personal success or failure. The numbers are the score card for the business and the entrepreneur. Emery and Ann lived Vanity, the business, every waking second of their days. Nothing was too small to be overlooked, and they were hugely successful.

Chapter 15

HOBBIES

In addition to exploring business opportunities, a well-rounded executive will usually have interest in non-business activities commonly referred to as hobbies. For me, my hobby is golf. I have great memories of many golf games, and love the time spent with friends and family outdoors. We live in a society filled with opportunities for personal growth and hobbies.

A good hobby can offer you great relaxation, and give you the common experiences needed to build friendships. A hobby will help you become a more well-rounded individual, resulting in greater personal riches.

Chapter 16

TEACHER'S IMPACT

Almost everyone can identify a teacher or two who has had a major impact on their life. During my teenage years, I was fortunate to experience two teachers who greatly impacted my life.

My seventh grade mathematics teacher, Mr. Tom Humphrey, opened my mind to the joy of teaching. As luck would have it, my school combined the seventh and eighth grade math classes, and Mr. Humphrey was chosen to lead the instruction. A short time into the year, Tom recognized my math skills and asked me to help teach math to an attractive eighth grade girl. I had never before been so motivated to study, be on time for class, and prove myself. I was thrilled to be considered intelligent enough to help an older student. The fact I was attracted to her just added icing to the cake. Eventually, she and I did arrange to meet at a YMCA dance for a date. Unfortunately, it was the only date we had together. We remained friends throughout high school, but lost contact after graduation.

As a result of this innocent young experience, I gained the desire to teach others my knowledge and I carry this desire to teach with me today. You, too, can help others gain the desire to share knowledge, and help others find riches in life through sharing.

Teacher's Impact

By high school, my desire to learn had been replaced by other activities. I struggled with English. During my senior year in high school, Mrs. Joan Humphrey (Tom's wife) entered my life. She, like Tom, recognized something inside me. I was once again inspired to learn. Morning after morning I arrived at Mrs. Humphrey's office before classes started to work on my English skills. She constantly encouraged me. Even today her words of encouragement echo positively through my mind. She constantly showed me how I could succeed at my weakest subject. Time and time again she would proclaim ; "You see, you can do it!" She did not give me false praise, but helped me learn by working with me each and every moment we were together. Undoubtedly, her impact on my life has created my desire to lead people to greater achievements. You, too, can inspire others by sharing your knowledge.

Chapter 17

TO MOTIVATE OTHERS

All people are motivated. You cannot motivate people yourself, but you can create an environment where a person becomes excited to achieve. Motivation only comes from within oneself. You can help people recognize their personal dreams. Maybe, if you are really good, you can help inspire people to reach harder for the achievement of their dreams. A key to remember is that all motivation comes from within the individual. You must want to achieve. To be a successful entrepreneur, you must have a burning desire to achieve business success, and have a constant, intense drive to win and succeed.

Chapter 18

MOTIVATION

Permanent motivation is the internal drive to grow and move forward. Sometimes a book, a speech, or an event can help create a temporary or a continually burning flame to help motivate a person.

Basically, there are two types of motivation. One is reward motivation, the other is fear motivation. Both have their place and either can create a strong desire within yourself. Either can lead to great accomplishments. Your preferred motivation style is largely dependent on your experience in life and what you deeply desire as an outcome for your life.

In my drive to rebuild my body, I use both reward and fear motivation. My reward talk is - Keep working and you'll be healthy again; and talk like - Look at what you can do now. The fear motivation is - If I don't keep up the gym routine I could lose my health again, a return to a wheelchair is not an exciting proposition!

Most of today's motivation experts focus solely on reward motivation. It's show up for work, do a good job, and you'll get a pay raise. The thousands of people pitching their retirement plans use reward motivation almost solely. They rarely talk of the possibilities of loss, only talk of the financial riches their subscribers will receive by investing with them. If only it were that easy, we would all be millionaires.

Reward motivation focus is effective, but in an organization, the rewards can only grow so large. Eventually a balance must be struck so the organization can prosper, grow, be profitable, and add new employees. I once consulted with a business totally focused on rewards. Only a few select employees had an opportunity to grow. The businesses survived, but it took years to get back on track. Over time the company president recognized the issue and designed rewards based on each individual's accomplishments. A good balance was struck. Eventually the organization became stronger, all employees were happier, and greater growth occurred over time.

Fear motivation, on the other hand, has it's place as well. It's the factor which says, work hard or you're going to get fired. This too works to an extent. Eventually people driven by rewards will find a place more conducive to their motivation preferences.

My experience with Texas Instruments was a perfect experience for a young man. I was a control manager (financial person) at Texas Instruments in the early 80's. I found Texas Instruments a great place to work, but most of the attitudes were against sales and marketing. Most of the financial people berated marketing. The engineering people responded by designing above specifications. To this day, I believe Texas Instruments' professional computer in 1983 was far superior to that made by anyone else of that day. Texas Instruments just didn't know how to sell it. Their motivation was not to sell, but only to design engineering superiority. Engineers were rewarded for superior design. Sales and marketing were always fearful of budget cuts, resulting in great products, but an unproductive work environment. Texas Instruments is a great company, and I would recommend it to anyone. It's easy to pick on one problem at any company, but it is hard to find a better multinational employer than Texas Instruments.

When I first started to recover from my stroke, a lot of fear motivation was used by the therapists. It went; if you don't get up and do these exercises, you will not get better, you might even die. This probably worked a lot better than approaching me with, don't worry, you don't have to work hard, a couple of aspirin and you'll be all better by morning.

I now go to the gym three times per week. I use a combination of reward or positive motivation, and fear. I tell myself, if I keep it up I'll get back to the strength of a normal person. If I slack off I could slide back and loose my gains. The combination is working, but hard to keep internalized. I wish I could use all positive reward motivation, but the time exercising is just not that enjoyable for me, so I use both motivators to keep it going. I focus on the end result of positive health, not the negative side of loosing ground.

Most of the successful entrepreneurs I know have an internal motivation or desire for success. Seeing your organization grow is one of the greatest feelings of self-worth a person can find in life. As I see our employees grow and develop their success in life, I get a great feeling of personal richness. The rewards and satisfaction of watching people grow are enormous.

As I review this chapter, one man stopped in to thank me for a recently earned pay raise. He explained how the raise allowed him one step forward so he and his wife were able to buy their first house. His earned reward and thanks made me feel fantastic. What a great sense of self worth to be able to help a man reach his dreams!

A true entrepreneur doesn't leave home in the morning to go to work. Each day is a new adventure filled with stimulation and fun.

Chapter 19

MOTIVATION EXPERTS

Today there are dozens of speakers who specialize in personal development and motivation. One cannot deny the effectiveness of people like Anthony Robbins and his personal power series. One of my preferred motivational experts is Zig Ziglar. I had the good fortune to attend one of Zig's seminars in 1978. His message rang true to me. Since that time I have relistened to his tape sets many times, read most of his books, and my wife and I have participated in teaching his philosophies at our company. I have found the personal rewards from using and following Zig's philosophy to be fabulous. Zig poses two great questions: Is it morally right to all parties concerned? And, does it bring me closer to my long range goal or further away? Just using these two questions can help answer many dilemma's one faces in life. I recommend you pick a personal, motivational philosophy you can live with and work to live by it.

Joan Lunden (of Good Morning America fame) has written two books about her life which are very motivationally directed. I am convinced she is one of the great motivational teachers of the future. Buy her books and read them!

Some people claim you should only use positive motivation. Obviously, only positive reward motivation will not work in the long run. Can you imagine the swimming coach standing on the side of the pool, telling the beginning swimmers how great they are as they slowly sink to the bottom? Of course, the right action is for the coach to jump in the pool, show the beginner the correct movements, and encourage only correct activity.

At one time we had a sales manager who could not face "negative" comments and only tried to use positive motivation with our sales people. As sales would lose ground, he would set targets lower and lower in order to provide positive rewards. Of course, the whole organization suffered, and people realized this sales manager was not capable of growing our business. One sales rep, after years of continued decline, was shown his poor numbers. He eventually left our employ feeling he had wasted his time. "Why didn't that sales manager tell me I was doing so horribly. No wonder I felt my job was a burden and not a pleasure," he said upon leaving.

I believe strongly you should praise people for performance, but it has to be specific and has to be truly superior performance to warrant high praise. False praise is worthless and usually recognized by the recipient as having no value.

You can't sit by the sidelines and tell a person they are doing great as they fail. Eventually, your false praise will show through as worthless. As the false praise catches up to you, you will have to answer the tough questions of why you were praising a performance which was actually poor. A good coach knows you only praise real progress.

One of Zig Ziglar's most famous philosophies is, "You can have everything in life you want if you will just help enough other people get what they want." A solid principle for a business owner.

At Dacotah Paper Co., one successful employee is Barbara Wegter. Barbara started with us as receptionist, then became a secretary, then moved on to be our Executive Secretary. One day she became my secretary full time. As the years progressed, she recognized the value in following Zig's philosophies while working with me. She demonstrated great loyalty and became my confidant. She puts into practice these philosophies and challenges me when I seem to drift away. I have countless examples of how, with Barbara's help, I achieved some desired objectives. One shipment from a vendor we agreed to a one-dollar per case promotional allowance. The vendor billed us one dollar per case instead of one dollar off; a ten thousand dollar error in our favor. Barbara caught the error and brought it to my attention. We notified the vendor of the error and paid the correct amount.

Before the Family Leave Act was passed, Barbara and her husband adopted a son. The riches I felt personally as she exuberantly explained she and her husband were finally approved and would receive their child were enormous. I followed by granting her

51

whatever amount of time-off she desired. During her time-off those first few weeks with her new son, we talked frequently and she did much work at home. Both of us getting what we wanted by facilitating the other person to get what they wanted. She had time at home, I had uninterrupted work flow.

Chapter 20

THE PEOPLE GROWTH FACTOR

Great entrepreneurs love to help people grow and prosper.

Helping people find prosperity in their lives creates great personal fulfillment.

It's often said that teachers receive their greatest rewards from watching their students succeed. Entrepreneurs receive fabulous rewards from assisting people to grow and succeed in life. I have a good friend who owns a large real estate firm. He has a natural talent for encouraging people and, as such, inspires them to achieve in life. When we walk through any of his facilities, he always takes the time to introduce me to a few employees. He always speaks about one of the individual's latest accomplishments when he introduces me to the person. A stronger and more motivated group of people is hard to find.

My father had a knack for inspiring people. I remember one particular sales person was struggling in a growing market. We decided to add a new person, thus cutting the existing person's account load. My father called the man explaining how the man was now going to really do his job better. The man was in his mid-forties, and sure enough, he took off and succeeded beyond our wildest expectations. My father had recognized and provided just the right amount of needed encouragement, and my father was mighty proud he had helped the man succeed.

Building people provides more riches than building the tallest structures in the world.

It's the entrepreneur's dream to watch people develop and to encourage their success.

Over the years, I have watched people acquire material possessions as a result of the rewards they received for a job well done. More importantly, I have watched many people grow in responsibility and blossom into great people. You cannot measure the joy one receives when an employee thank-you note is left for you at the office which provides thanks for helping someone achieve their goals in life.

Don Gill, our Information Technologies Manager, is a great example of a person who wanted to grow, wanted to lead, and has succeeded with our organization. Don is a very bright and computer literate person. When he first joined Dacotah Paper Co., he became very frustrated, and expressed his frustration to me. We had such great hardware, but yet we allowed ourselves to let the software lag. He wanted us to utilize our assets and talents better. After a couple of employees left, he asked me to give him a chance to grow. Don is not your average pen-in-the-pocket computer guy. We talked on multiple occasions; what could he do to learn more about the whole company? Today he has a major impact throughout our whole company. Long before the hype of the year 2000 issue, Don began addressing our system's preparedness. He constantly asks how a change will better enable us to serve our customers or save us money. His excitement and his good attitude is reflected in everything he does. Additionally, on a personal note, Don now strives to take a few hours each week to attend his son's football games, which occur during work hours. He also has brought his daughter to the office for Father-Daughter Days. He now has this flexibility in his work schedule to give extra time to his children. Don carries a real sense of personal riches as evidenced by his career success and his devotion to his children's success.

Leao Erfle, another super successful person, started with Dacotah Paper Co. as a young man in our warehouse. Soon he moved into the office, then to major account sales. Leao has no post high school education, yet he is an extremely valuable part of our company. He handles a major portion of our business completely on his own. Over the years he has grown in authority and responsibility. I have never met a person who didn't like Leao or appreciate his work ethic. Many outside our company think he must be a member of the family. In a way, he is and he feels he is. When my brother quit, he asked why would a member of the family quit? I reassured him my brother preferred to hunt and fish rather than work. Leao recalled how my brother had indicated he felt Arizona was a better place to live than Fargo, and so, in a way, he expected him to leave eventually. In a sense, Leao takes events at Dacotah Paper Co. personally. As an example, on Friday before Memorial Day, we were notified of an opportunity to enhance profits through a special purchase with a vendor. Leao was planning a weekend with his family. The next week I was booked, so Memorial Day, he and I came into the office and worked together for the afternoon. We learned from each other that day. Our business and everyone benefited. Leao is a key success component for us.

Chapter 21

PREPARATION

Success in life involves commitment and the diligence to be prepared for success and be prepared for failure. Any sports enthusiast knows you have to practice, practice, practice to get prepared for the game. You have to be prepared if you think you are going to win. Sometimes events occur, like my stroke, which you cannot be fully prepared to deal with.

Despite the fact I was not fully prepared for a major medical issue, I was reasonably prepared to handle the effects of a major illness. I was in excellent physical and mental condition. My wife and I had a strong relationship built on love and with a God-centered family philosophy. Mentally, when we were married, she decided she would be prepared to handle anything. Due mostly to her strong faith in God, we have maintained our relationship through these trials.

As an entrepreneur, you need to mentally rehearse for business events. What do you say and do if a fire devastates your business? As the designated company media spokesperson, I have mentally practiced many catastrophic events, helping to prepare us for most situations.

One situation I should have been more prepared to handle was my brother's resignation. Deep down I think the family all knew he would be the first to leave the company. His departure was probably long overdue, but my emotional state caused primarily by my stroke threw me for a loop when he quit. I was fully prepared to handle the business. Our people were strong, I had solid relationships, and felt I could depend upon the group. Decisions about who should do what came easy. Yet, I cried like a child. I should have been thrilled; no more arguments about how ideas wouldn't work out. No more blaming people long since gone from our organization. It was a time to allow much deserving people room to grow. Most people were prepared to move ahead, most were excited about the opportunities which would flow to them, and we were all ready to succeed.

Fortunately, my assessment of our strength as an organization was correct and we continue to grow and achieve new levels of success. In his absence, little to nothing has gone undone. Our people were ready, and most stepped up to the ladder of success. Sometimes no level of mental preparation is enough, but there is no doubt mental preparation will help when reality strikes.

Chapter 22

READ TO GROW

Through reading this book, I hope you have gained knowledge and can use my experience to enhance your life.

By reading, you learn to expand your experiences, and become more valuable to society. As your value to society increases, your financial rewards increase.

Everyone should have a personal library where books you have read and refer too are kept. A book doesn't enter my library shelf until I have read it. Reading provides a great escape, as well as enhances learning.

If you could earn an extra million just by reading a book, would you read it? What would happen to your life if everyone else read the book, made the million, and you missed the book! Read, read, read.

Chapter 23

BEST ENTREPRENEUR SKILLS

The top skills an entrepreneur needs to succeed are accounting/finance, marketing, and human relationship skills. You can never have enough ability in these three areas. Your approach does not have to model someone else's. Maybe some people don't agree with your management style. That doesn't make it wrong. It is what you accomplish that matters most. Perhaps you like to use fear motivation. Does that make you a bad manager? Absolutely not, but fear tactics will probably fail with reward-motivated employees. Work on your finance, marketing, and relationship skills first.

Chapter 24

PERSONAL RELATIONSHIPS

A hard-driving entrepreneur often has difficulty maintaining deep relationships. When constantly asking for superior performance of yourself, it is easy to see the faults in others. As you come to rely more and more on someone, their mistakes or errors in judgement become personal, so the confidence and enjoyment you have in the relationship can become weaker.

Through my deep desire to succeed in my business, I have burned through a number of relationships. Some losses I regret, others I realize were for my best.

When I first became married, I went into the marriage with the same drive, determination, and goals for success I would do in a business project. Unfortunately, I kept my business priorities on top along with my marriage, which added undue stress to our marriage. My wife has a deep commitment to God, which gives her strength. We are fortunate to enjoy a great life, and have built a wonderful family of five. But, I admit my drive for success and riches has hurt our relationship.

When our first child was born, I went into parenthood with huge drive, determination, and lofty goals for the little fellow, and expected top fatherhood from myself. With no other reference point, my first son and I grew a deep relationship together. We have a magical relationship which has brought great riches to both of our lives. I continue to work to develop the same magic with our other two children.

Today, I have built a terrific relationship with my second son, and he is constantly building his life towards success. With my daughter, it is too early to tell how she will respond to my drive, determination, and be-the-best attitude.

Consequently, I feel compelled to suggest you carefully examine your spouse and commit to the relationship you each desire. You can have both a great business and a great family. Much will depend on how you define your goals and work as a family to achieve these goals.

Becoming uninterested in your partner's daily activities is a quick way to destroy a relationship.

Every night I make a point of asking each member of my family about their daily events. I am sincere in my interest, and, with two grade-schoolers, I receive some pretty funny replies.

Chapter 25

GOALS

Having significant goals is critical to personal success, having goals for your business is even more important for business success.

Goal planning is a relatively simple process. First, one needs to decide on the end result (the goal). Then, when you want that result (the achievement date). After deciding what you want to achieve, you need to set a time line with intervals which provide smaller goals or steps you need to take on your journey to the main goal. Without goals, an organization simply wanders about the economic landscape. One set of goals every business should keep is revenue goals; how many dollars of sales is the target? An even more meaningful set of goals is the number of people planned to be employed at an enterprise.

If your organization in general generates $10,000 in sales per employee, if you set a goal of having $1,000,000 in sales, a corresponding goal is to employ 100 people. Personally, I think a 100 person company is a significant business. Part of the great fun of being an entrepreneur is providing more and more economic opportunities for individuals.

I have been setting my goals since the late 70's. Each year I break my goals down into six categories: physical, spiritual, mental, career, financial, and family. Writing down one year goals, five, ten, and long-term goals helps clarify purpose, and I believe firmly that goals keep you on track to achieving greater accomplishments.

A brain injury doesn't allow one to heal "normally." The brain is not like an arm or leg, so when the brain is injured, everyone responds differently. However, the brain does heal over time. I am cautious to be certain to set realistic goals for myself, but I go through the experience of setting goals yearly anyway.

First I walked three minutes on a treadmill at 1.5 miles per hour. Gradually I increased the time. I then set a goal of 10 minutes at 1.5 miles per hour, then 10 minutes at 3 miles per hour in 30 day's time, then 30 minutes at 3 miles per hour in 60 days. The walking I accomplished rather easily. Slowly I keep working on my hand and arm, which are not responding quite so easily. I have to be careful to set realistic goals so I don't discourage myself. Goals need to be big and they need to be achievable.

The size of your goals is very important. Goals need to be big to have meaning, but they have to be achievable to inspire action. For example, you may have a great new software you've developed. Your goal may be to become larger than Microsoft. Certainly, that's a big goal, and if the software is good enough, your goal is achievable. But to overtake Microsoft in six days is probably ridiculous. Can you imagine someone trying to hire employees by explaining they were going to beat Microsoft in six days! People, in general, would run away in laughter.

After you have set a goal with a date for accomplishment, you need to identify what resources you need to acquire to achieve the goal. Then determine a plan of action to acquire these resources and a plan of action to use them to achieve your goal. I also believe written goals produce greater results.

Looking forward, one can find excitement in fulfilling dreams and goals.

Looking backward, one can only remember.

Look back, remember and understand, then turn quickly, look forward to what life's wonders can present to those willing to take a chance at living.

The future is bright for those willing to look beyond yesterday's sunset.

GOAL PROCESS:

1. Decide on your goal.
2. Set a date when you will have succeeded in achieving your goal.
3. Evaluate needed resources.
4. Acquire the resources you need.
5. Put these resources to use towards your goal.
6. Write your plan down and review it periodically.
7. Work your plan and set bigger goals with each accomplishment.
8. Enjoy your success.

Chapter 26

BE WELL ROUNDED

You will notice goals are meant to give a person a rounded life. One cannot truly feel rich if they are not building a successful life with all aspects of life attended. For me, it means being better physically, mentally, spiritually, financially, in relationships and in business.

Quoting the bible: "What profit a man if he gains the world but looses his soul?" You need to build everything and keep a good balance to life to feel deep riches.

You probably have guessed by now that I feel God intended us to be rich in our lives. After all, God did give us life so we could enjoy life abundantly. I have little question in my mind that God gave us the opportunity for riches so we didn't have to squander life in poverty.

Chapter 27

FROG-WISE

This story is a little different from the writings of the rest of this book, but I thought it had particular relevance right now. I hope you enjoy the lesson it teaches us.

Sitting on his lily pad, a wise old frog noticed a beautiful maiden walking by the stream. He thought how wonderful it would be to be kissed by that maiden, yet it was comfortable on his lily pad, so he decided not to risk the long swim to shore.

A short while later, he noticed another frog jump from his lily pad, swim to shore, and sure enough, the maiden leaned down, picked the frog up, and kissed the frog.

Suddenly, the frog who had swam to shore turned into a prince and walked hand in hand with the beautiful maiden toward the king's castle.

The wise old frog then turned toward the setting sun on his lily pad and thought to himself, I wonder what would have happened if I would have swam to shore? Oh, well, he thought, it's nice and warm here on my lily pad anyway . . .

Take a chance on life today!

Chapter 28

WORK HOURS

Of the dozens of super successful business owners I know, all of them share one common trait. That commonality is the continuous drive to work and be involved. There is no such thing as a forty hour work week for the true entrepreneur. Weekends are filled with business activities, oftentimes with much time spent at the office. Full days off rarely occur.

My father was what you would call the classic workaholic. I rarely saw him; most of my memories of time with my father are our times together at the office. Although, my parents did buy a home on a lake for weekend relaxation, we did buy a power boat, took many leisurely boat rides, and I water skied nearly every weekend. However, most weekends my father and I would start each day at the lake talking about business, and generally would carry our business conversations on late into the night.

One can argue much of my medical challenges have resulted from my drive and determination to succeed in business. For the 23 years preceding my stroke, I worked an average of 80 to 100 hours per week, not one hour of which I would change today.

My wife quickly learned that a vacation simply meant we didn't sleep at home, I didn't go to the office; but she also learned every day had at least two hours on the phone checking messages, following up on issues at the office, etc. After I was able to secure computer links long-distance with a lap-top computer, each vacation day starts by "dialing-in" and ends the same way. You can surely assume I can't be much of a husband with my great love for business.

Work is fun for the real entrepreneur. Most of my business associates can be found at their offices at all hours of the day. One day a venture partner of mine came to a meeting rather tired. He apologized and explained he woke up early, then drove to the office to do some extra work so his family could sleep undisturbed. Upon arriving at the office, he discovered it was 2:00 A.M! The entrepreneur has an undeniable enthusiasm to be where the action is. Certainly, families suffer, the individual's health suffers, but it's all fun for the true entrepreneur.

I have concerns for today's new business owners. One concern is far too many of these new business owners held forty hour per week jobs before venturing out on their own. Many feel pressured by any small amount of overtime requirements. A true business leader looses sight of the 40 hour week early on during the days of business development. If you don't have the drive to spend countless hours working, how can you expect others in your organization to put forth extra hours of effort?

Chapter 29

THE NON-WORKING SPOUSE

I was fortunate to grow up with a mother at home. Although my mother didn't work outside the home, my father included her as part of our business. My mother always had a good sense of what was going on with Dacotah Paper Co.; she contributed her ideas and helped guide my father with the decisions he faced. Now, a few years after his death, my mother is actively employed by our company as a director, resulting in a continuity of thoughts and ideas.

My wife was professionally employed before the birth of our first child. After our first child was born, we made the decision she would be a stay-at-home mom. Despite the fact my wife is now not professionally employed, I encourage her participation in our business endeavors. Early on in our marriage I paid for her to attend a training class to learn the teaching mechanisms for a Zig Ziglar philosophy based attitude program. Afterwards, she and I team-taught a number of these classes together at Dacotah Paper Co.

Today when I hold employee meetings or company events, I encourage my wife's attendance and often request her to participate.

Although she is not on the payroll, her presence at these events, I feel, signals to all employees we are truly a family business. Her presence, I believe, provides an added linkage for employees.

When a spouse or children are visible at the business, their presence shows to all involved that the business is part of your family. Today, in addition to involving my spouse, I encourage my children to romp through the hallways during off hours when they accompany me to our offices.

My personal riches are greatly enhanced when my children, wife, and mother can be comfortable at my office. With my mother now active in our company, I have the great pleasure of sharing our ongoing success with her.

During our building years, my father always included recognition of my mother and gave her much deserved credit for his success. Even now, years after my father's death, my mother brings dozens of Christmas cookies to the company for all the employees to enjoy the week prior to Christmas. Her cookies arriving are a major event to all the folks at Dacotah Paper Co. A personal touch that goes miles to say everyone is appreciated and considered part of the family.

Chapter 30

BUILDING

To be referred to as a builder of people is by far the greatest accomplishment a person can receive. In our world, monument builders receive much attention. Creating desire, inspiration, and success in one individual provides a sense of riches which exceeds the height of the tallest structures in the world. When you combine building people with building structures, it's magical.

My son, Caleb, loves to help with household projects. Over the years, together we have built a ping pong table, shelves, and worked on many fix-it-up projects. When a job is completed and he knows he has had a hand in its creation, his eyes shine with excitement. I'm not much of a home handyman, but together with Caleb, any small project successfully completed gives us both a great sense of personal riches. Maybe it is a little early to tell, but I think he is showing the signs of becoming a great builder. He inspires me to achieve, teach, and learn. He inspires his other little friends as well. My personal internal rewards have been immense as I have watched him grow.

A person is never too young to get involved with building people. Helping others grow is a great source of personal riches.

Chapter 31

YOUNG CHILDREN INVOLVED IN
THE COMPANY BUSINESS

Legally, I joined Dacotah Paper Co. a few days before my sixteenth birthday; though I had been employed (paid) for various duties for nearly two years prior to actual legal permanent employment. My father allowed me to join him at the office at a very early age.

My father taught me how to run our computers, gave me jobs cleaning windows, cutting our lawn, cleaning light fixtures, and washing trucks.

Prior to my illness, my two oldest children (then ages 5 and 3) would join me each Saturday morning at the office. I feel this helped teach them hard work was a component of success, and gave them a level of comfort in our business surroundings. Today, each of them feel completely comfortable in all areas of our business and know many of the employees by name. Now, as I am able to work some Saturdays, the boys join me at the office for more time with their dad.

Young Children Involved In Company Business

After one particularly successful year, I purchased a big box of candy bars and had my oldest son, Benjamin, then about four years old, personally walk through our facilities and give each person a candy bar and say, "Thank you for making this last year such a great success!"

This candy bar exercise, I believe, helped imprint upon his developing mind two very important factors. One being each person helps us succeed, and when we do succeed, everyone should be rewarded. A full sized candy bar is a big reward for a four year old. Most employees thanked him for the candy, so he received a double dose of positive reinforcement through the exercise.

Based on my experience, I believe any age is the right age to start the learning process of the family business. Your children should be familiar and comfortable at your business. But, your business is not your child's babysitter. Learning and understanding are the key components to children's involvement. Let your children know work is important and work is fulfilling.

Certainly, one of my purposes today is to perpetuate Dacotah Paper Co. so one day, should one of my children wish to continue the endeavor, they will have that opportunity. As you probably can guess, I look forward to the day I present one of my children with the title of President of Dacotah Paper Co.

Chapter 32

DONATING

The easiest thing to give is money. Time, on the other hand, is much harder to give to community organizations in need.

My experience on various community boards has been both educational and rewarding.

I was lucky in that my grandfather gave a tremendous amount of time to our community's development. He was at one time the chairman of the Fargo Chamber of Commerce, he worked for the development of local public services, and was well respected throughout our community. His public service gave our company great exposure and much publicity. My father rose to the heights of an Eagle Scout, became a scout leader, and he developed a great network of business associates through the years. My father did serve on a local bank board as an outside interest. His bank board experience was a great time of learning for him, and our company benefited from his experience with the bank. My father rarely forgot a person or their interests. I can remember marveling at how my dad seemed to know something about everyone of importance. It's no wonder why the bank solicited his support. My father would relate stories to me about businesses which succeeded and those that failed, who was involved and why.

As a result of my grandfather's community involvement, I was immediately accepted as a local leader. My father supported my every interest and helped guide me with his knowledge of the people and organizations I helped.

The exposure our company received over the years from our community service has been phenomenal. Some of our best growth years can be linked to times when we were most involved with our community.

One caveat to giving time: You must be sincere and do the work. Everyone quickly recognizes the joiner who doesn't give efforts for a project's success. If you are not willing to commit, don't be a joiner. By just showing up and not doing anything, you are worse off than not being involved at all. The people involved almost always resent the tag-a-longs, the do-nothings!

On the other hand, I do not believe in donating time to profit making business organizations. If you are asked to serve as a director or consult for a business, you should be paid. Early on in my career, I agreed to help a couple of businesses in an advisory capacity. I quickly realized most of the other un-paid supporters did little to help the enterprise. Most didn't even read the materials we intended to cover at the meetings!

My wife has a passion for religion. One year we decided we should teach Sunday School. Then she suggested we volunteer at another church for a young children's Christian program called Awanas. In both cases I thought this was her thing, not mine. For the benefit of our marriage, I decided to tag along. As with any thing I get involved with, I gave it my best effort. Soon I loved interacting with the children and doing my best to teach from the Bible. Today I still miss these particular activities and interactions with young children. These are both good examples for me about being involved and truly donating of oneself. Had I not put forth my best efforts, I would have missed a great deal of joy and the feelings of great richness which the children provided me for my time teaching.

There are countless opportunities to become involved within any community. Being involved and actively working for the good of the community helps everyone involved. You and your business are recognized, you learn about people and the community in which you live, and, as a result, your feeling of personal riches is greatly enhanced. Show up, tag along and do little, and you are bound to be frustrated, disappointed, and viewed as a failure or slacker. Get involved, get interested, do the work, and you will gain riches in your life.

Chapter 33

FAMILY

Family takes on a whole new meaning when you consider a business enterprise. As a new business begins or your enterprise matures, you need to define who your family members truly are. Obviously, your spouse, your children, your parents, and your siblings are family members. But yet, with the business enterprise, there are family members that you really would not quite recognize from outside of the enterprise.

ADOPTED FAMILY MEMBERS

Adopted family members are those people who work for your organization and give their heart and soul to your business as well as supporting the family in many many ways over the years. Rather than you truly adopting them, it is more that they adopt you. They are the people that are there on the front lines for you, fighting for whatever goals you set out, and trying to keep the family members all appraised of what is happening within your business. It can be the accountant, or it can be the customer service agent that has been with you for 2 years or even for 20 years, it can be the truck driver or warehouseman. It's the people that volunteer to help whenever you need help. They are the people that are there for you in all different times.

In my opinion, as these people have adopted you as part of their family, you need to adopt them as part of your family. Their goals, their desires, and their livelihood have to be part of your conscious thought upon each decision you make for your business enterprise. Are you providing for these folks with a long term security as well as your blood family members? Are you providing these people a way to expand their horizons and find some fulfillment within your organization on a daily basis? Every year are you challenging them with new tasks? To forget these adopted people is no better than to forget your own family members themselves, because they are the heart and soul of the truly successful family business enterprise.

The successful entrepreneur takes into account his own family and the many many other people that have adopted him and that he has adopted over the years. The successful entrepreneur finds a way to meet everyone's needs along with serving his customers in the best way. In almost every circumstance, you will also find that these "adoptees" are on the front line. Oftentimes other employees do not quite understand that these people have been there for years serving customers, allowing the organization to grow. And so most business owners are under tremendous pressure to eliminate these people by outsiders who come in and provide counsel to the business owner, these people seem more like dead weight or rusty anchors around the owner's neck.

Outsiders rarely recognize the long-term employees for the significant contributions they have made over the years. These adoptee's tend to look played out and unable to handle the new challenges each business enterprise faces every year. Unfortunately, by eliminating some of these adopted family members, businesses fall victim to a lack of continuity or a perceived lack of caring develops with the remaining younger employees. Employees often feel that the business owners are not adequately meeting the employees' needs. Adopted members have been through so many battles and learned so much about how to make things happen within the organization. As they are replaced by younger or less experienced people, the organization suffers in immeasurable ways. The little things that matter to the customer may be forgotten, the personal touch of knowing what the owner wants gets lost, and other seemingly insignificant, but important aspects of the business get lost. The adopted family members truly make part of the family business enterprise a successful endeavor.

This section would not be complete without mentioning a few of our most valued employees. Employees who, in a way, I considered have adopted me.

As I learned our business, we employed Gary Rodacker as our warehouse manager. He taught me as much as he could about warehousing. In my teenage years, he would push me to work harder, gave my employment reviews, and assigned me duties; all knowing one day I could be his boss. Fortunately for me, Gary is not a man who is intimidated. He taught me freely and openly whatever he thought was best. Today I consider him one of my most valued allies. When I was hospitalized, I considered who I could call and ask to take me home. I had maybe six or eight people I felt would come and rescue me. Gary was on the top of the list. Through countless personal trials, Gary has always supported me and my family and our business objectives.

Recently I did an out-of-the-box employee performance review. One question I posed to myself was, "If I were going to war against an enemy with machine guns, but I only had a shotgun, would this person join my platoon?" I had no question in my mind that Gary Rodacker would be on the front lines with me, so he naturally received the highest "performance score" on this question. It's the kind of faith and belief in each other which is rarely found in the world today. I know Gary supports me totally, and I believe he realizes I support him completely as well. I also know, should a shotgun versus machine gun situation occur, with Gary on my team, my chances of success are greatly multiplied. I have the faith that he would lead the shotgun charge and overcome any enemy. Gary is the kind of man who made our country great.

Over the years Gary Pedersen, currently our Vice President, has watched our business and our family grow and change. He is a top rate accountant. He joined our company in 1978. After a short while he became a director of Dacotah Paper Co. Through the years he watched as I struggled to wrestle control of our business. Regardless of the issue, I always felt he gave me an honest answer. Prior to my brother's departure from the company, I asked Gary to review my performance and assess my brother's performance. His comments to me about each of our performances were all encouraging, but not all positive, so I knew he felt he could be direct and honest with me. He did tell me that I was considered by all employees to be the company's leader, and he felt the position for me as leader was the correct one. Less than 24 hours later, he voted as a director to endorse my brother's resignation, essentially to support me as the company's only leader. Certainly, a circumstance no one wishes to be put in during their lifetime. Gary was honest, forthright, and helped guide a decision which had a major impact on my family and Dacotah Paper Co.

A third individual in our organization who is undoubtedly one of the family is Roy Lemke, a salesman for Dacotah Paper Co. since 1967. Roy has grown throughout the years and has always been a great supporter of our company by helping others to learn and encouraging new sales people to succeed.

An example of Roy's personal character came to light in November 1995, approximately one month before my father's death. My father had missed a sales meeting, so Roy called my father to chat about the meeting. This phone call and Roy's interest in my father's opinion provided some of the happiest moments of my father's last days. Roy is a man of great character, a person who anyone would be proud to associate with.

I hope these examples give you a glimpse of some of the great benefits and rich rewards working in your own family enterprise can give a person through the relationships which can develop.

Chapter 34

GOOD-BYE TIME

Certainly there is a time in a person's career or in a relationship when it becomes time for them to move on or be moved on. Handling employee departures is probably my hardest task. Every failure in our business I take as a personal failure. I ask myself, "Why couldn't I have helped and guided this person to success?" What resources would have assisted this person to succeed with us? Unfortunately, not everyone succeeds at everything. I feel a deep desire to allow people to grow and provide pathways for continuous success. This is one of the family business's most endearing traits.

When employees seem to be failing, I've always tried to encourage new growth opportunities for the individual within our company. During my career, I have had to suggest many discharges, but only once have I personally had to let someone go. The individual was a computer programmer unable to do her job. The discharge was not a surprise to anyone, yet I handled it. Years later, I still often ponder what I could have done to help her succeed.

It is very hard for me to accept employee failure. At one time we had a sales person who initially succeeded, but then after over 20 years, he started loosing ground. Years passed as one account was lost after another. I sent multiple messages to our then sales manager. Finally, in a heated argument with our sales manager, I explained, "It's no longer a matter of waiting - you must do anything and everything to help him succeed, even if it means going into the field and selling for him." The sales manager replied, "I've tried, there is nothing which can be done." The sales manager's attitude, of course, I found unacceptable. The sales person stayed with us and the sales manager continues to be unemployed.

Chapter 35

FAMILY GOALS

The enterprise must serve customers, yet it must continue to meet the ever-changing needs and desires of your family. Before becoming involved in a venture, ask the question of how this venture will help all family members reach their goals and provide the lifestyle they each desire. It simply will not work if family members are expected to contribute to the enterprise, but are not included in setting the enterprises goals.

Later, I recount an example of my brother-in-law, Les. He wasn't included in long range goal planning. If he would have been, I'm certain he would have contributed and felt much better about his position with the company and our family.

FAMILY MEETING

Since much of my background deals with strategic marketing and planning, one of my early tasks was to develop for our board a formal strategic operating plan. While developing the strategic plan, I requested input from all family members and our board. Early plans were very successful, but the updates became less committed to. By the time of our second and third plans, I felt a distinct lack of commitment by our board, primarily due to one board member's lack of interest. As a consequence of this lack of commitment, the success of the second two strategic plans were far less than our first plan.

After my brother quit, I decided I needed to return to using my strengths in planning. We built another strategic operating plan, and I shared it with those involved in it's execution. The strategy has been working wonderfully well and we are succeeding with our plan, and, as a consequence, our business is on track for stronger growth.

One way to clearly establish goals for an enterprise which will be cohesive among the family is to hold a family meeting, where all affected family members are asked to specify their goals. At this meeting, you want to determine what they would want should they choose to become involved. Certainly not an easy task, but effectively run, a family meeting can lead to cohesive goals and bonding of purpose. If left uncontrolled, such a meeting can turn into a disaster with arguing and bickering. Essentially, a waste of time. In my organization our board meetings often take on the flavor of a family meeting. As Chairman of the Board, I suggest philosophical changes, restate our corporate principles, and seek to gather support as well as conviction from all participants, and encourage input from all involved. I view this as a necessity of my position. I strive to insure our ideals remain intact for future generations.

Since I have the background and experience in creating cohesive family plans, my approach to the family plan has been to talk directly to each family member and determine their personal objectives and desires. I speak with my wife about what her preferences would be as the business leader's spouse, as well as her concerns for our children in the business. I always make a point of asking my mother her desires to try to determine her comfort level. When my grandfather, father, brother and brother-in-law were involved, I poled them as well. With this information, I then pull together everyone's needs and desires and work to craft a written plan to achieve as many of the objectives as possible. Through this process, I have gained the satisfaction of realizing my mother is secure, and my brother achieved his dream of not having to work. My sister and her family are very happy (despite their stressful departure from our company), and I have the leadership position with the business I have always wanted. Certainly, a sense of personal riches I have found in pursuing each family member's objectives in this way.

Chapter 36

FAMILY HIRING DECISIONS

As your business progresses and even at the beginning of your business formation, a critical decision you need to address is whether or not you will allow family and/or friends to be employed with your firm. It's very easy to start off by offering opportunities to a family member or friend, but such decisions are often made without giving thought to the long term affects on the business.

As you look to your decision to start a business enterprise, you should immediately address whether or not your spouse will become involved with the business. Some husband and wife teams have created incredible enterprises. Some, however, find it very very difficult to work together. You have to know each others strengths, must be able to leave family issues at home, and not bring home matters back to the business.

The issue deals with; "Do you hire relatives?" Everyone has heard the story about the family relative that has ruined the business, be it the uncle or the cousin or the son-in-law, etc. etc. I have some direct experience in this regard, which created some interesting times for our business and family. As it so often happens, when we started to enjoy some ongoing success, my brother-in-law, Les, was working for a paper distributor in a different area of the country. One of our seasoned sales people planned to retire, so why not interview Les?

I was fortunate to have my father's confidence, so when the company management group met to decide, nearly everyone, fearing to oppose my father, suggested we give Les a try. I quickly recognized this groups lack of commitment. My statement at that first meeting was, "It can not be a matter of trying, Les must succeed." During our family discussions, my mother also recognized a lack of commitment to success and she asked if we were sure Les was the right choice - did he really want to work in North Dakota? Did the company have a plan? Who was going to insure his success?

You probably already know the result. After struggling with little to no help from our then sales trainer, we recognized Les needed to be moved from his sales territory. Then Les came to the Fargo office to help develop new business. He was well liked, but we offered him no clear career pathway. He hadn't grown up in the business, so he was lost with no direction.

By the time I was fourteen, I had decided to work for the family firm. By sixteen I openly stated I wanted to run the business. My brother found sales his calling, so he learned that part of our business.

We had great hopes and dreams of big success for Les in our organization. Unfortunately, in desperation we turned Les over to my brother, hoping together they could secure some new business and create success for both of them. With no direction, no authority, and no plan, they floundered for over a year. Neither were happy or producing for the company.

After multiple unsuccessful and ambiguous projects, one holiday Les's frustration hit the boiling point; the decision was made that Les needed to move on. My point in this example is: Here is a bright, well-liked family member who failed because of the lack of a clear pathway. If we would have listened early on or created a family-member policy, much grief would have been spared the whole family and business. Les's departure from our family firm was extremely hard on both my father and mother as well as my sister.

My suggestion is to decide up front if you want to include family members. Decide if one person is going to be in charge or if you want to attempt shared duties amongst the family members. One family member almost always translates into all family members who need a good job!

On the other side, working with family members can be exciting and very fulfilling. If you are a parent, think of how rich and blessed you would be to have your children join you every day at the office for a fulfilling career together. My own experience working

Family Hiring Decisions

with my grandfather and my father, helped me enjoy my life much more than I otherwise would have working for someone else.

93

Chapter 37

CHOOSING A LEADER

As I ponder my family business and others which I know of, the question arises who or how do you choose the leader? I believe the leader of a family business is one of the most stressful positions one can aspire to, yet the leader is usually self appointed. It's the drive, desire, commitment, and interest which propel the right person to the top. In my case, ever since I was a teenage boy, I would profess to any family member that I intended to be the majority owner and President of Dacotah Paper Co. some day. I studied the business and only accepted top performance out of myself and the company. From an early age I loved spending time in our warehouse and working with our computers. Fortunately, my father encouraged me. I was keenly interested in how everything worked, and my father loved telling me about how he did his work or figured out how to do something.

Over time, I became more thrilled with my leadership position, and I speculate my brother became more frustrated having to accept my authority.

I get a great feeling of riches as I am able to help others achieve their dreams, and, for me, that's what leadership really represents. I do believe true leaders share with others and encourage and teach others personal values as well as business information.

Prior to my father's death, I had the chance to learn from him every day. Anything I wanted to discuss, personal or business, he would take the time to listen and share his insight. Only by working together with my father, would I have had such a rich amount of time with him.   Otherwise, I probably would have hardly known him, or him me. I was lucky in that my father loved to teach.   He generously shared his knowledge with me at all times.

Chapter 38

OWNERSHIP AND CONTROL

Most family advisors today believe that only one family member should be given control of the business. Easy in theory, difficult in practice. The emotions of the family, and the misguided belief that your family is somehow different, often leads business owners to fracture their company amongst their children.

My story is a classic example. Working for the company since I was fourteen, I knew I wanted to be in control, and own Dacotah Paper Co. My father encouraged my participation and taught me well. I bought stock in the company at an early age. Soon, between myself and my two siblings, I owned the most shares of the company. I boldly predicted I would own 51% of Dacotah Paper Co. one day. My brother was working for the company as vice president. I was vice chairman and chief operating officer. One night my brother claimed, "I always wanted to own the company, too!" My father and mother faced a new level of distress, since each of us were treated equally. Eventually, through buying the voting stock of non-family shareholders, I acquired over 51% of the voting control. After a diligent study of family business, somehow I deluded myself by thinking we could be an exception to the normal family business. Nontheless, I insured I had voting control of the business. My brother resented being only a minority shareholder, and expected he would be given his chance to buy stock equal to me. Only I made efforts to acquire stock. My brother waited for me to include him, but took no action on his own. My drive for ownership did create some unnecessary stress in the family, but regardless of the stress or conflict created, I wanted to have control of what I considered my company. There was no question in anyone's mind who would eventually end up with control of Dacotah Paper Co., by ability, ownership, drive, and desire. Of course, today I do own controlling interest and the greatest number of voting shares in the company, my brother has sold all of his ownership in the company, my sister has retained her ownership, and my mother continues to hold a large ownership stake in the company.

Chapter 39

AN EXECUTIVE

To become an executive or to be recognized as an executive is a great ambition, one which exceeds the ambition or desire to be a manager, an owner, or the president of a firm. Not everyone has the personality of an executive. When one thinks of an executive, one considers traits such as confidence, polish, and sophistication. The buddy-buddy manager can never raise to the level of professional executive.

An executive needs to have strength, courage, control, and the ability to make the hardest of decisions. Most people recognize the difference between a business manager and a business executive. A true executive knows when to stand firm, when to turn back, when to praise, and when to apologize.

As you develop your persona, you need to visualize yourself as the owner, the boss, the manager, or the business executive. Undoubtedly, a business chief executive is the business leader. The business manager may not be the business leader. Certainly, the chief executive garners more respect.

Chapter 40

A GOOD REPUTATION

There's an old saying which goes, "You can't do good business with a bad person."

Everyone has a reputation. For a business owner, a reputation is a critical component of long-term success. Reputations transcend generations. For me, I was lucky my family and business has had the long standing reputation of being honest, hard working, and loyal to our friends, employees, and customers.

Today, the best motivational-personal development experts have segments of time devoted to personal integrity and building a positive personal image. A reputation, once earned, usually sticks around for years. I'm sure you can list a few businesses which you avoid because they are dishonest, or at least you learned from someone how the business person who owns it is of questionable character. We all must protect and build a positive reputation both in our personal lives and in our business dealings.

When I was going to purchase my first new automobile, I recalled my father's story about how a certain car dealer had mistreated him when he went to buy a new automobile in 1960. The man insulted my father. My father then walked across the street and bought a new Buick station wagon, despite the fact he initially intended to buy a different brand.

When I had enough money saved to buy myself a car, I decided I would do the shopping by myself. Since I was very independent, I decided I should give the dealer who offended my father a chance to see for myself how he would treat me. I asked to see the sales manager. After he learned where I worked, he then spoke poorly of my father. I walked out of that showroom, never to return. The dealer probably lost a chance at over 500 new automobile purchases since 1960. He sure kept up the reputation he earned with my father.

Chapter 41

ON CHARACTER

The definition of personal character I like best is, "Character is the ability to carry forward with a resolution long after the mood in which the resolution was made has left you." I translate good character to mean continuous commitment. Always doing what you say you're going to do, always following through with your plans and statements.

I pride myself on being a man who is true to his word. I refuse to suggest even a casual lunch with someone unless I intend to follow through. In short, I don't believe in good intentions, I only believe in doing what I say I'll do. Most of my better friends understand this quality and many unknowingly follow it themselves.

If someone casually suggests lunch with me, I generally respond with something to the effect that it would be nice, or I respond with, call me next week or so. If I haven't been contacted by the person within two weeks, I know the depth of the person's character. If I respond with, let's have lunch or I would like to have lunch soon, I most often follow up on the suggestion myself, since now I consider the event my commitment.

On Character

Does following through with a simple lunch suggestion mean anything about your character? It absolutely does. Assume you are invited over for dinner to a friend's house. After the meal you casually suggest one day you will return the invitation and meal. If you let it pass or forget about the reciprocation, does it matter? It probably doesn't matter unless that friend remembers your lack of reciprocation. Essentially, by not returning the favor, you just placed yourself in the category of the average man. People always make unintended suggestions, but only people with a true depth of character make commitments, not suggestions.

If you want to be known for your superior personal character, don't make well-intended suggestions. Become a person of commitment in everything.

Chapter 42

ON FRIENDS AND BEING SOCIAL

A true friend is there when you are on the top, is there with you when you fall, and is with you on your way down in life. Put another way, a friend is the one coming in to see you when everyone else is leaving. Or, similarly, a friend is coming in your door as others are leaving.

Since I was very young, I had always been a "social" person. I was involved with many activities, enjoying the interaction among people.

My wife claims my definition of friendship is much less than hers. Whereas her friendships, she claims, are much deeper than mine. One of the worst decisions which was made for my benefit was to not allow visitors or the use of the phone while I was hospitalized. Consequently, I felt socially deprived. A few of my friends managed to get by the nurses with a phone call; one friend waited for six hours to see me. If that isn't true friendship, what is? Finding myself without the social contacts I was accustomed to, I engaged conversation with anyone who would talk with me. The poor therapists and hospital staff who listened to my never-ending talk about how great Dacotah Paper Co. was, and about my wonderful children. If someone would listen, I would talk!

On Friends and Being Social

As you can guess, those few friends who made that extra effort to see me or even to call me in the hospital are very important to me. I favor them with business and, given the chance, I brag about their abilities, and even defend their weaknesses when necessary. These few good friends didn't let me down when most everyone else had written me off, and I am not about to forget their friendship.

Of course, in retrospect, the deprivation of my social life slowed my recovery and had a terrible impact on my attitude.

Shortly after my hospital discharge, my wife and I attended our high school class reunion. Of the 365 graduates, I claimed to know about 360 of them. By then, I was walking with only a small brace, so I received much encouragement from my old classmates. It turned out to be a very positive experience for me; a return to my social self. As the night passed, I recognized my attitude getting better. When asked as I was leaving how I was, I replied, "I'm great!" and meant it. Being social for me was and is good, worthwhile, and positive.

I now realize that one internal measure of my subjective feeling of wellness or richness involves my being involved with other people on various projects or activities. Jim Gargiuolo is one person whom I had worked with as a director of Network Services Company and Network Associates, Inc. Jim is one of the brightest and best businessmen I've ever met. Before his recent move to Florida, he ran a successful enterprise in New York. Over the years, Jim endured countless questions from me about how to better run a business. I used as many of his ideas and suggestions I could in my business endeavors. I can not think of one suggestion he gave me which did not work out for me. Without a doubt, much of my business success can be attributed to Jim's unselfish sharing. He was one of the people who repeatedly tried to contact me and offer me encouragement while I was in the hospital and after I returned home. I know I could call Jim with any trouble or problem I faced and he would lend me a helping hand. Not only a true friend, but a man of superior character.

As one ponders life, certainly the number and quality of friends we have helps us measure our sense of self worth. I feel rich when I am allowed the opportunity to learn about people, their lives, their dreams, and desires. I use my social interactions as a great learning tool, a way to explore life through others' experiences.

An interesting situation occurred recently when my wife and I saw one of her old friends. The person recognized me, but had no clue as to my name; then saw Cynthia and did not remember her name either! The person's spouse showed up and, of course, the person suggested we all get together for a meal. I didn't commit, but suggested that they call us when it was convenient in their lives, but they never called us and we didn't call them. So much for that deep friendship!

Business friendships can be meaningful and rewarding, if you make the effort to grow together. I have two great friendships that have grown directly out of business relationships. One is with Jon Strinden, a great lawyer; the other with Jim Wieland, a real estate developer. In both cases, we have owned businesses together, and golf frequently together. We do socialize with our families, and, fortunately, both of these men know I have complete faith in their abilities and I consider them great friends.

My experience developing my local group of venture capitalists provided excellent rewards concerning personal and business friendships. I consider each member of the group a good friend. We come from diverse backgrounds, and all run successful enterprises. We have a variety of educations, and are diverse in our interests. When I decided to sell my stake in Vanity, all the partners supported my decision and sold their shares with me. We have fun, share our life experiences, and work together to enhance our lives.

Chapter 43

ON RELIGION

The interweaving of religion is evident in all areas of a successful life.

Personally, I always felt I had a strong religious upbringing. I strive to keep the right balance. People in our organization who needed to profess their faith were allowed to, but we did, very early, develop a religious harassment policy.

Too much preaching rarely works. Everyone views God differently. My philosophies don't fit for everyone. Of the few business owners I know who try to demonstrate their great religion and boast of their deep commitment to God, I have heard stories of each of them being dishonest to customers and mistreating employees. Naturally, people ask what this person is trying to hide. I once consulted a religious book store to help them develop better marketing efforts. The owners were deeply convicted to God, but in their business dealings they didn't try to preach the gospel. They simply did what was right. After a few years (only partially due to my help), the business became very successful. In part because the owners found the right balance. They didn't preach, but they demonstrated their spirituality by doing what God would expect.

On Religion

My wife can be characterized at times as a religious fanatic. Throughout my illness her faith provided her an inner strength which showed through to all around us. I have deeply admired her commitment to God and the strength she has gained from her convictions. Although we don't share the same level of faith, she doesn't judge me, and I work to understand her.

One of the biggest mental struggles I faced after my stroke, and to an extent still face, is when I ask God, "Why God, did you do this to me?" Certainly not the right attitude, but a natural outcome of major health failure. My faith does tell me God must have had a good reason. Certainly my life has changed, but a lot of my life is better because of my stroke. My desire to enjoy life is higher, the values I place on personal relationships is higher, and I have found a deeper sense of personal riches in my life. My wife and my mother always help calm my soul when I get discouraged with God's allowing my stroke to occur.

The right religious balance can add great richness to life. My suggestion is simple; if you feel the need to preach to others, go to a seminary and become a minister. If you want riches, find a balance of prayer and thankfulness to God for your gifts.

Chapter 44

ON COACHING

While I was hospitalized, starting therapy, I would frequently ask the therapists; "Who's the most important, the player or the coach?" Few had much of an answer. Certainly, without good coaching, athletes would never become professionals.

In therapy, I was more than determined to walk; even though the medical staff felt my walking ever again was unlikely if not impossible. Finally, one early Saturday morning Christi Teigen, my therapist, suggested we try something new. She wrapped my foot and ankle: two steps later I had defied the odds! Now, after months of work, I walk with minimal pain, and can even jog 30 minutes on a treadmill and do a slow jog around our block where we live. No coach, no walking for me.

One of the greatest coaches I have ever seen in action is Jim Alexy, my friend and president of Network Associates in Mount Prospect, Illinois. Jim has a natural talent to teach and motivate others to learn. A great deal of my passion for golf comes from the times I spent with Jim on the links. One particular round I struggled with multiple sand shots. Jim suggested we spend 30 minutes practicing together. After 10 minutes of his instruction, 10 minutes of my practice, followed by 10 minutes of Jim praising my correct practice shots, I started to love hitting from the sand. Even with only one functional arm, sand shots are often my best. Of course, Jim's great coaching spans far beyond the game of golf, it is evident in his successful leadership of Network and shows through in his excellent relationship with his wife and their children.

When my brother quit Dacotah Paper Co. I called Jim looking for some guidance. He gave me many encouraging words and helped settle in my mind that my brother's departure was really for the best. I consider Jim one of my best friends, and a personal confidant of mine. I know that for any crisis in my life, Jim will stick by me and give me any help he can. A true friend, a great coach, and a man of impeccable personal integrity. To be able to consider Jim my friend gives me great feelings of personal well being, or riches.

Chapter 45

TAKING CARE OF OUR OWN FUTURE

While much of this book speaks to the issues of business success, and taking care of people/family during times of crisis, I haven't addressed the issue of our aging population itself.

One of the great benefits of a family business is having the resources to take care of the elder members of your family long past normal retirement age. Certainly, the comfort and confidence one would gain from knowing that your needs will be met by your family, in your later years, can lead one to a much higher level of subjective well-being or the feeling of richness during one's lifetime.

My grandparents are perfect examples of how a family business can meet the needs of loved ones long into their elder years. As a result of my interest and knowledge of finance, and my commitment to doing the right things regarding my family's care, I was given the responsibility to take care of my grandfather's personal affairs, and eventually, after his death, the responsibility of arranging for care of his wife. My grandfather never took large sums of money from the company, but instead invested wisely and lived a modest, comfortable life. When he died, my father was still living, and my grandfather knew that should a financial need arise, my father would take care of all the needed expenses. Similarly, he had fully briefed me on how he wanted his wife's life to carry on. He died knowing I would insure his and her wishes would be carried out. Although he didn't die a financially rich man, he certainly died with great confidence, and a rich soul.

My mother is a remarkable woman. We have had a very close relationship since I was a child. My father wanted to insure and feel secure of her lifelong enjoyment. He often asked me to take care of her when he was gone. I assured him I would, but as fate may have it, with my stroke, she more takes care of me than I do of her. She provides me counsel, guidance, and strength. When issues arise, she always does her best to help me. If it were not for the family business, I am certain I would be in a warmer climate working elsewhere. The business called me home from my pursuit of a career with Texas Instruments. Part of my personal sense of richness comes from being able to interact with my mother in her elderly years. I am very lucky she is very sharp mentally and enjoys our interactions as well. What a great situation for both of us to continue to grow older and closer through a common company/family legacy.

You could argue that it's unfortunate our family relationships have so much business involved. Yet, without it, and with me miles away, how good would the relationship become?

Today my mother participates in business meetings, and travels with me for business purposes. Often I will pay for my wife and children to join us, allowing personal time for my children to be with grandma. My mother attends most meetings and we share ideas.

I gladly pay my wife and children's expenses for these travels. Every business trip I take, I am thankful for the riches I am provided with, by allowing me to be with my family and being able to expand my horizons and grow my business acumen.

Chapter 46

YOUR CHOICE

Everyone in our great country has the choice to live a successful life. I hope by reading about my experiences and through learning my philosophies, your life will be enriched. Certainly, by now you believe a lifetime of riches is available to you. As you complete your first reading of *Personal Riches and Entrepreneurship*, I hope you are inspired to follow your dreams to achieve the life you desire. Enjoy a great life, and take a chance on yourself today!

Chapter 47

FURTHER SUGGESTIONS

1.   Buy and read a current addition of "See You At The Top" by Zig Ziglar.

2.   Write down a set of your top 10 goals today.

3.   Follow the goal-setting procedures in Zig Ziglar's book.

4.   Buy and read "A Bend In The Road Is Not The End Of The Road" by Joan Lunden.

5.   Enjoy your success every day.

Success is not for the faint of heart, but success is reserved for the strong and courageous among us.